D1789392

The School and Small Business Computer, Server and Network Guide

The easy to understand guide covering configuration, recommendations, and specification information for Windows computer systems and networks.

Steven MacRory

Contents

About This Book

The aim of this book is to provide a thorough guide that clearly explains everything that you need to know to set up a Windows computer environment. Covering the Setup and administration of Windows Server 2016 and Windows 10 this book is presented in clear and easy to understand language.

The book explains: the purposes, specifications and roles of Windows Servers and how to correctly configure a server; PC specifications and how to configure them to join a Windows domain; Computer networks and networking specifications; Licensing for Windows; Anti-virus options for small to medium-sized organisations; tips and suggestions on setting up the right system whilst considering budget restraints; and a section on certification recommendations and interview preparation for IT technicians.

Audience

This book is for anyone that would like to gain the knowledge necessary for setting up and configuring Windows computers and servers for use within an organisation or educational establishment. It is primarily aimed at new technicians, school employees or business owners looking to develop their computing systems, or anyone looking to become an IT technician. It may also assist people that are studying towards Microsoft server certification.

Introduction

I have spent the past 6 years as a computing technician working within a large junior and infant school. During that time I have completely redesigned, installed, setup and configured the entire system. In addition to this, I have put in place a backup system and redesigned the school website.

I have a degree in web design and I am Cisco and Microsoft trained. Despite this much of my training and qualifications go into too much depth for what is required to set up a small school or business IT system. I have yet to find a guide that is straight to the point, put simply, with everything in one place and in a logical order. That is what I have aimed to do with this book.
I hope that you find the information helpful.

Servers

What are Servers and What Are Their Uses?

A server is a specialised computer designed to run various and different tasks when compared to an ordinary computer.

Uses will vary and will influence what the specification required. However, the main purposes for a server within small to medium organisations are:

- File Sharing – the use of shared folders that various people can access in order to save, edit and share documents.
- Printing – Sharing of printers.
- Controlling who can log on and what they and the computers can and cannot do.
- Controlling the computer IP addresses (DHCP).
- Installing software and updates to computers on your network.
- Increased file and network security.
- Increased reliability

You may require it to do more, or less, than the above list. These are points to keep in mind when approaching a sales company and discussing your budget. Also, bear in mind the future proofing of your server. As technology moves forward, file sizes usually increase and you may want additional functionality such as mail server capability. Choosing the right server will become clearer in the next sections.

Types of Server

Most suppliers will provide good advice on the type of server best suited to you. However, it is always useful to know what salespeople are referring to. Below are the main types of servers and their uses.

Windows Home Server

This may be a suitable option for a small organisation or a few (less than ten) office computers. Useful for file sharing, data storage, and backups. It is easy to set up and relatively inexpensive.

For the majority of school environments, this would not suffice. However, it could be used in addition to the main server as storage for a particular department or office if required.
You would connect to and configure this type of server via a remote connection through the network from your PC.

Network Attached Storage (NAS)

NAS in some respects is similar to Windows Home Server with the main differences being that it does not use Windows and will usually include additional capabilities such as Virtualisation and web hosting.

They are usually Linux based but will feature an easy to use front end interface usually accessed from a web-browser on a PC via a network connection.
They usually include a number of bays so that additional Hard-drives can be added as required.

The main uses would be file sharing, data storage and the backing up of data. Consider this option if you require a simple solution to additional data storage space.

Tower Servers

Whilst Tower Server and Blade Servers can and do utilise various operating systems, for simplicity we will be focusing on Windows Server Systems.

Tower Servers usually resemble a large desktop PC in appearance and will usually be physically located on a desk. Micro-Towers are a smaller option. Tower Servers are generally priced somewhere between a NAS and rack-mounted systems. A monitor, keyboard, and mouse are usually required to access it.

A Tower Server running Windows Server Software is capable of numerous tasks and has a variety of capabilities. Unlike the Servers previously mentioned a Windows Server has the ability to provide varying levels of control over the PCs in your domain using various software and tools such as:

- Active Directory – This is used to control the users and computers that access your domain. We will see how users and computers are added later.
- Group Policy Management – This is used to set the rules/policies that are applied to the users and computers. For example, you may wish to set a policy that places a specific image as a desktop wallpaper on certain computers.
- Print Management – This can be used to install printers which can then be managed centrally and shared with other computers.
- Windows Server Update Services – Updates can be configured so that they are controlled by your server rather than all the computers on your network consuming your bandwidth by updating over the internet.

- Shared Folders – Control who can access specific folders that are set up for collaboration.

Please note that Windows Servers are capable of much more. For the purposes of most initial setups in smaller organisations and schools, these will be the primary uses and the ones that we will be focusing on.

Upgrading the specification of a tower server is usually very easy. New hard drives can easily be added for additional data storage. If purchasing a tower server I would recommend that you have spare hard drive slots available for future expansion.

Consider this option for larger environments where you require centralised control over users and computers, you have limited physical space and you are unlikely to require more than 2 or 3 additional Servers.

Blade Servers

Much of what applies to Tower Servers applies to Blade servers the main difference being that they are designed to be mounted inside a chassis. The advantages of this are that new servers can easily be added by simply sliding it into the chassis and the chassis can house a variety of equipment such as networking equipment. The chassis provides cooling, power and data connectivity meaning that no additional cabling is required. They are neater and provide more computing power for the physical space required when compared to Tower Servers.

The downsides are that its initial cost is higher due to the fact that a chassis and its installation is also required. It is usually more difficult to upgrade blade servers. However, hard drive space is usually external to the server so this will not typically be an issue if more data storage is required.

If you have the physical space, budget, requirements for more than 2 or 3 servers then blade servers would likely be your best option. Also, consider this option if the organisation is likely to be seeing significant expansion and additional requirements in the near future.

Purchasing a Server – Things to Consider

You may be posed with a number of questions and options when it comes to purchasing your server. When it comes to obtaining quotes contact a number of suppliers and get as much information as you can from all of them. Explain your requirements and ask them all for advice on what server specifications they think will be best suited to your organisation.

The following information is designed to provide you with an overview of some of the options that may be available to you in order to help you make a decision.
Also, try to negotiate extras and play the suppliers off against each other. I have always ensured that I have had the RAID configuration and Operating System installed by the suppliers at no extra cost as a minimum.

It is also worth noting that many suppliers do not include the cost of the operating system in their quotes. Ensure to check this and read the chapter on Licensing for further information.

Type of Server Hard Drives

The most common hard drives for Windows Servers are Serial Attached SCSI (SAS) and Serial ATA (SATA). Generally speaking, SAS is faster and more reliable whereas SATA is slower with higher capacity and cheaper.

SAS will usually be used in environments where high speed and reliability are crucial such as banking. SATA will usually be used for less demanding roles such as data storage. That's not to say that SAS should not be used in your organisation. My personal preference and choice are SAS. However, the budget at the time permitted this and I was tasked with making our system as fast as it could possibly be. One option could be to use a combination of the two. With SAS disks used for the Operating System and SATA disks used for data storage.

RAID Configurations

RAID stands for Redundant Array of Inexpensive Disks. The Server or NAS will likely include some hardware called a RAID controller. If it does not, RAID software is also available. RAID is mainly used for fault tolerance. If RAID is configured hard drives, depending on the type of RAID can fail and the Server will continue to run. The faulty hard drive can then be replaced without losing data.

There are different types of RAID and choice is affected by the number of hard drives, performance required, whether the device has the required hardware and how much fault tolerance is needed.

The main types of a RAID are:

RAID 0

RAID 0 requires a minimum of 2 disks. Data is written across multiple disks which increases performance as the work that the computer is doing is handled by more than 1 disk. RAID 0 does not provide any fault tolerance.

RAID 1

RAID 1 requires a minimum of 2 disks. It is relatively low cost and is the simplest way to implement fault tolerance. It is often referred to as 'Disk Mirroring' because data on one hard drive is copied to another. This way if one hard drive fails the others can keep working as both disks contain the same data. The disadvantages of RAID 1 are that it reduces server performance and it halves the total disk capacity. So, if a server with two 1TB hard drives is configured with RAID1 it will only have 1TB storage capacity.

RAID 5

This is the most common type of RAID configuration for NAS devices and Business Servers. It provides fault tolerance with better performance when compared to RAID 1. RAID 5 can tolerate the loss of a single hard drive disk and the disk can then be replaced without having to shut down the server (hot swappable). Data is striped across all the disks (a minimum of 3) and if one disk begins to show errors the data is copied to the other disks. RAID 5 uses parity to achieve this. Parity is additional data which is used for this recovery process.

The main drawbacks are that it is slower to write to the disk compared to RAID 1 as parity data also has to be added. RAID 5 configuration also means that the capacity of one of the disks will be lost. For example, if you have 3 x 1TB disks, the total capacity for data will be 2TB.

RAID 6 is similar to RAID 5 providing further reliability as it stores an additional parity block meaning that 2 drives can fail at once without breaking the array. It is mainly used for file storage servers and the main drawback is lower performance due to the additional parity.

Other RAID levels are really variants of the above and are usually only used in specific circumstances. These include 2, 3, 4, 6, 7 and 1+0. For most small to medium-sized organisations 1, 5 or 6 would be a common choice. An important point to remember is that RAID should not be used instead of a backup strategy.

Hard Drive Storage, RAM Size, and CPU

Unfortunately, there is no 'one size fits all' guidelines, but options will often be restricted by cost limitations. The obvious advice is to suggest purchasing the best available for your budget. However, the following information should help you make a choice.

The main points to consider for hard drive sizes are:

- **The number of users** – Obviously the more users you have that will be saving to the server the more storage space you will require.

- **Types of files that users are likely to be storing** – Consider what people will be saving. Word processor documents and presentations will generally not require as much storage space as video, music or image files for example.
- **What you will be using the server for** – You may want to utilise the server for email for example in addition to general storage.

Assess how many users you have and consider the amount of storage that types of users will require. For example, some people that use their computer all day every day will require more storage space than users that login on occasionally to check e-mails for example. Consider future growth and expansion.

RAM or Random Access Memory is where the data that the Server or computer is currently working on is stored. So a computer will load a file from its storage into its RAM. Generally, more RAM means that the Server will cope better with more tasks simultaneously.

Problems arise with RAM when it fills due to too many tasks being run at the same time. It will then start to read and write to the storage disk which slows it down significantly. Therefore, to maintain performance it is important to have enough RAM.

The CPU (Central Processing Unit) or Processor performs calculations and controls other parts of the computer. Many people liken it to the 'brains' of a computer. The speed or clock rate is measured in hertz (Hz) or more commonly these days in gigahertz (GHz). Generally, the more gigahertz a processor has the faster it will be and the better your computer or server will perform.

Operating System

Operating systems are a type of software that runs on a computer and manages the memory, processes, hardware and any additional software.

Because servers are used differently and provide numerous users with varying services they require a server-specific operating system. Linux based servers are often preferred by expert system administrators and are usually free. However, most users and administrators in schools or small businesses are much more familiar with Windows interfaces. In a school environment where computers are shared and different users are logging onto different computers regularly then the server will need to run Active Directory. In which case, Windows Server is the only choice. For the purposes of simplicity, we shall be focusing on Windows-based servers in this book.

Assess your main requirements and prioritise your budget. For example, if storage of files is your main concern ensure that you will have enough hard drive space. Also, consider the following points.

- Ensure that if you purchase a tower server it has additional slots to add extra hard drives if required.
- Ensure that the Operating System is installed on a separate hard drive (or Drives) to data storage.
- Ensure RAID is configured.
- Remember that capacity is significantly reduced when RAID is configured.
- Check with suppliers on what RAM and processing power they would recommend for your requirements.
- Ensure that your quote includes an up-to-date Operating System and any other required software.

- Ensure to ask your vendor about any warranties that are included or available. These can vary significantly and may be really useful in the future.

It can be difficult to decide on a budget before you know the costs. The way I approach this is to first contact three reputable suppliers and request quotes based on their recommendations. I would then look at the specifications suggested and from the information above and the costs begin to put together a specification that I would be happy with. I would then go back to the suppliers requesting the second quote with my exact specification.

Another option would be to ask a single supplier for 3 quotes. A 'budget' quote, an 'ideal' quote and another somewhere in the middle. It is also a good idea to contact other schools or businesses in the area. Ask them about their computing suppliers and experiences.

The minimum requirements Microsoft recommends for Windows Server 2016 are:
- 1.4GHz Processor
- 2GB RAM
- 32GB storage to install the Operating System

I would suggest a minimum of a 3GHz processor, 8GB RAM and 100GB of Hard Drive space for the operating system.

Windows Server 2016 Configuration

Server Name and IP Address

Once you have successfully purchased, installed the latest server operating system, connected the peripheral devices and the Ethernet connection the server will require some initial configuration. These are set using the Server Manager.
Server manager allows you to administer settings and add additional bits of software called Roles. Server manager will start automatically when the server is fully booted up.

We are going to change the computer name to something more meaningful and set a static IP address. In order for other computers to locate your server, it is important that it maintains the same IP address known as setting a static IP address. If you are unsure what your IP address should be we can initially set the same settings that the server has been assigned via DHCP. Go to start -> run and type cmd. The command prompt window should open. Type ipconfig in the command prompt window and make a note of the IPv4 Address, Subnet Mask, and Default Gateway.

1. In **Server Manager** locate the Local Server option in the left pane. Local Server refers to the server that you are logged into rather than a remote server.
2. In the main pane next to Computer Name click the current name of the computer to change it. A default name will have been set by windows.

3. Click the **Change** button.
4. Delete the existing computer name and enter something more meaningful such as 'primaryserver'.
5. Click **Ok**, Close and **Restart later.**
6. Adjacent to Ethernet0 click the current IP address.
7. Right click on the Ethernet port and select **Properties**
8. Click Internet **Protocol Version 4** and select **Properties** at the bottom.
9. Select **Use the following IP address** and enter the IP settings.
10. Select **Use the following DNS server addresses** and enter the DNS server (leave this as automatic for now if you are unsure). Click Ok and Restart later.

It is also worth having a look at some of the other settings here and configuring them to your own preference. Such as Windows updates and the Timezone settings. Once complete restart the server.

Installing Roles and Features on Windows Server

Software components of Windows Server are separated. This means that we can install certain parts of the operating system to perform the services that we want. For example, if we would like the server to manage our IP addresses using DHCP we can install the 'DHCP Server' role. The roles often supply a service such as Active Directory, File, Print, DNS or DHCP. If we can save a file to a server or if we can send a print job to a server, then that server is running some software that is enabling us to do those actions. Using separate software components for the roles aids efficiency as the server is only doing the tasks and processes that we require.

Features are added bits of software usually required for the roles to function correctly. The correct features will usually be selected automatically after you have selected a role in the install wizard.

To install a role:

1. Open **Server Manager**
2. Click **Manage** located towards the top right corner of the screen.
3. Select **Add Roles and Features** to open the wizard.
4. Click **Next**.
5. Select **Role-based or feature-based installation** option and click **Next**
6. Select the server you would like to install the role on. There is likely to be only 1 server option, the one you are currently working on, click **Next**
7. Select the role that you would like to install, add the required features and click Next
8. Click to confirm the installation and wait for the **installation complete** confirmation.

Windows Domain

The Domain networking option is built into Windows computers and is used to create a group of computers that can be controlled centrally from the server. A domain also makes a network more secure as it can block traffic from accessing computers in the network.

Once a computer or user is added to the domain they can access specified shared folders, files, software, and printers. When added to the domain computers will automatically be added to Active Directory and then rules or policies can be applied to the computer from the server. For example, you may want to set a desktop wallpaper or set specific desktop icons (more on this later).

The domain is initially set up on the server using the Active Directory Domain Services role. Computers on the same network can then be added. A domain requires a domain controller which controls login authentication of computers and users. If you have a single server environment then that server needs to be set as the domain controller.

In order to achieve this firstly follow the instructions for installing a role and select the Active Directory Domain Services role. Once the installation is complete there will be an option to Promote this server to a domain controller below the progress bar. Select this and follow the instructions below.

1. Select the option to **Add a new forest** (if this is your first or only Windows Server), type in your domain name and click Next. Note, Domain names should be simple without any special characters. Include a '.local'. Eg mydomain.local.
2. On the Domain Controller Options Screen:

- Leave the **Forest Functional Level, Domain Functional Level and domain controller capabilities** as the default options.
- Enter a **DRSM password**. Keep this safe as you will need it in the event of an emergency.
- Click **Next.**

3. On the DNS options screen ignore the warning, leave the tick box unchecked and click Next
4. On the Paths screen leave the default settings and click **Next**
5. Click **Next** on review options.
6. The server will now check the prerequisites. There may be a few warnings but these should be ok as long as you have the option to click Install. Review and click **Install**.
7. The server will reboot once the install completes and you can then sign into your new domain.

You can check that it has installed correctly by opening Server manager and ensuring the AD DS role is listed. You can also go to 'Tools' at the top right of the Server Manager Screen and open Active Directory Users and Computers from there.

Active Directory users and computers

Active Directory is used to store and group user accounts, computers attached to the domain and other peripherals such as printers, these are known as objects. The objects are stored in folders known as Organisational Units. For example, you may have 4 organisational units such as Staff Computers, Student Computers, Staff Accounts and Student Accounts. Different settings and rules can then be applied to the different organisational units.

Groups can also be created and objects can be added to the Group. An example where this would be used is for shared folder security. Within the Student organisational unit, groups could be setup up such as 'Year 1', 'Year 2' and 'Year 3'. Shared folders can then be configured that only allow specific groups access to them. You may, for example, have a folder called 'Year 1 documents' that you share with the group 'Year 1'. This way only user accounts that are members of the 'Year 1' Group can access the 'Year 1 documents' folder.

In this example, we will create an Organisational Unit (OU) and name it 'Office Staff'. We will then add a user object to this OU. Lastly, we shall create a Group called 'Office Staff Shared folder security group' and add the user to this Group.

Create an Organisational Unit
1. From **Server Manager** select **Tools** from the top right and scroll down to **Active Directory Users and Computers**.
2. Click the domain name in the top left to expand the drop-down menu and view the Organisational Units.
3. Right-click the domain name and go to **New** to open the sub-menu and select **Organisational Unit**.
4. Name the OU 'Office Staff' and remove the tick in **Prevent Container from Accidental Deletion**. Only remove this tick if you are following along for learning purposes and wish to

remove the OU at a later date. Best practice is to leave this box checked. Click **OK**.

Create a user or Object within your OU
1. Right-click the newly created OU. Scroll to **New** and select **User** from the sub-menu.
2. Enter a name and a user login name. Click **Next**.
3. Create and confirm the password for the user. Select the options in the tick boxes that best suit your organisation. Click **Next** and **Finish**.

Create a Group
1. Right-click the newly created OU. Scroll to **New** and select **Group** from the sub-menu.
2. Name the group 'Office Staff Shared folder security group' or something relevant.
3. Select **Global** for the group scope and **Security** for the group type if not already default. Click **OK**.

Add a member to the Group
1. Open the **Group Properties** page by double-clicking the group or right-click and select **Properties**.
2. Click the **Members** tab.
3. Click **Add**.
4. Enter the User's name that was created earlier and click **Check Names**. Once the name is underlined indicating that it has been located click **ok**.

In this tutorial, we have created an OU, a Group and a User Object. Bear in mind that as you add more to Active Directory (AD) it can rapidly become very untidy. Create a structured plan of how you wish to organise it. Individual preference usually dictates how your AD is organised but the tips below may help.

- Use separate OUs for different types of Objects. For example, ensure Users are stored in a different OU to Computers.
- Create a separate OU for Groups. That way they are easy to locate and don't get lost in a huge list of Users.
- Remember that OUs are just like folders and OUs can be created within other OUs. Using a school as an example you could have the OUs 'Office Staff', 'Teaching Staff', 'Teaching Assistants' and 'Management' all within the OU 'School Staff'.

User Profiles

In order to understand what settings are required for your user accounts, it is important to understand the different types of user profiles and their purposes.

In basic terms, a user profile is a folder containing a user's personal files and settings. Every user that logs on will have their own individual profile containing things like desktop icons, internet favorites and their files and documents.

There are 3 types of Windows profiles for you to consider when implementing a Windows network. Local Profiles, roaming profiles, and mandatory profiles.

Local Profiles

Local profiles are created and stored directly to the computer and are the default setting in Windows. You will have likely used this type of profile many times when logging onto a home Windows computer.

As the settings and documents are stored locally they can be accessed when disconnected from the network and any network issues will not affect a user's ability to log in and access their documents. Local profiles are specific to the computer so if the same user logged onto another computer the settings and documents would not be available.

Local profiles would typically be used where the same user is logging onto and using the same computer on a regular basis. For example, an office worker may be the sole user of a computer at their desk. Another example would be a user that requires access to their computer when it is not attached to the network such as a laptop that someone takes home.

Roaming Profiles

Roaming profiles are created on the server in Active Directory. When a user is logged on with a roaming profile and saves a file to their Documents folder it appears to the user as if they are saving to the computer on which they are logged on. However, the Documents folder is actually located on the server and this is where the file will be stored. This way when the user logs off and logs back onto another computer within the domain the same file will be accessible in their Documents folder.

Roaming profiles allow the user to login to any computer within the domain with the same settings, features, and access capability regardless of which computer they use. It is primarily used so that whatever computer the user logs into, they get the same desktop, mapped drives and saved documents.

Roaming profiles are extremely useful in situations where a number of users require access to computers and their files but they do not have access to the same computer each time. For example, imagine a school situation where different groups or classes intermittently use a computer suite. A roaming profile would mean that any student could log on to any of the computers and be presented with the same desktop experience.

When a user logs on with a roaming profile the profile is copied from the server to the user's computer and when they log off the profile is copied back to the server. This can become a drawback as it can increase network latency as profile sizes grow. As more or larger files are saved by the user login times will increase. The solution is to use folder redirection. Folder redirection allows the administrator to specify folders that are not to be copied across during the login process. The folder and files remain on the server but appear to the user as though they are stored on the computer they are using.

I would recommend using folder redirection as it will significantly improve log on and log off times. Instructions are provided in the section 'Set rules for users and computers in group policy' as folder redirection is configured in Group Policy Management.

Mandatory Profile

A mandatory profile is similar to a roaming profile. However, it prevents users from making any changes to settings or from saving anything. This is because the profile is copied to the computer during the login process but it is not copied back to the server when the user logs off.

An example where this might be used is with a guest or temporary account. You may wish to provide a user internet access only for example. The easiest way to create a mandatory profile is to create an Active Directory User object and apply rules to it using Group Policy Management.

Group Policy Management

The Group Policy Management role requires installation. Follow the tutorial on Installing Roles and Features on Windows Server and select the Group Policy Management Role.

Group Policy Management primarily allows you to manage settings for users and computers that are within the domain. When a setting, or group of settings, are configured in Group Policy Management they are called a Group Policy Object or GPO. Note that more than one setting can be configured within a single GPO.

Group Policy Management automatically synchronises with Active Directory and will display the Organisational Units created. GPO's can then be applied to specific Organisational Units. Note that a GPO cannot be applied to single Active Directory Objects.

Imagine a scenario where you have a number of computers in a specific location or room. Within that room is a single printer and you would like these computers only to connect to that printer. The computers could be placed in their own Organisational Unit within Active Directory. A GPO could then be created to install the printer and the GPO could then be applied to their Organisational Unit.

In this tutorial, we shall create a GPO that specifies how much time must elapse before the screen saver is launched. We shall then apply the GPO to the OU that we created in the previous chapter.

1. Once the installation is complete open **Group Policy Management**.
2. In the left pane click the domain name and open the drop-down list.
3. Right-click **Group Policy Objects** and select **New**. The New GPO window will open.
4. Give the GPO a suitable name such as 'Screen saver timeout'.

5. Click the arrow to the left of **Group Policy Objects** to expand the drop-down list and browse to the GPO that you just named.
6. Right-click the GPO and select **edit** to open the **Group Policy Management Editor** Window. This is where various settings can be configured for your GPO.
7. By expanding the drop-down lists in the left pane navigate to User **Configuration | Policies | Administrative Templates | Control Panel | Personalisation**.
8. In the right pane double click **Screen saver timeout** to open the settings page.
9. Click **Enabled** and set the number of seconds to your desired duration, eg 900 seconds for 15 minutes.
10. Click **Apply**, click **Ok** and close the **Group Policy Management Editor** window.

The GPO has now been created and can now be applied to Organisational Units. To do this follow the steps below.

1. In the left pane of the **Group Policy Management** click the domain name and open the drop-down list.
2. Locate the Organisational Unit to which you would like to apply the GPO.
3. Right-click the Organisational Unit and select **Link an Existing GPO....**
4. Select the Group Policy Object that you would like to apply by its name eg 'Screen saver timeout'.
5. Click **Ok**.

As you may have already noticed there are a huge number of potential settings that can be configured in Group Policy Management. It is beyond the scope of this book to list and explain every setting and their uses. I would advise you to familiarise yourself with Group Policy by browsing through the settings and getting to know how they are organised.

The easiest way to implement them is to list what you would like to achieve such as; prevent access to C drive; Map a shared folder; Force the web browser to open with a specific web page; prevent access to Control Panel. If you can't find them in Group Policy Management go on to utilise a search engine as the solution will almost certainly be on the web. For example, the search 'prevent access to C drive using group policy management' will highly likely provide you with instructions on where to find the settings to create the correct GPO.

Implementing Folder Redirection

Folder redirection can significantly improve system performance and login speeds. See the previous chapter for further information on user profiles and folder redirection.

Follow the steps below to configure folder redirection. Firstly we need to create a shared folder on the server so that Users files can be stored and retrieved from it.

1. Open a root drive on the server by clicking the **File Explorer** on the taskbar. Select the root drive where you would like the data to be stored by double-clicking it. Note that a root drive is the uppermost drive of a partition. If you do not have any partitions then it will be C drive.
2. Select the **Home** tab at the top of the pane and click **New Folder**.
3. Name the folder appropriately such as 'Folder Redir' and press enter.

4. Right-click the folder, click **Share** with and then click **Specific people**.
5. In the File Sharing box click the drop-down arrow and select **Everyone**, then click **Add**.
6. Click the drop-down arrow for the **Everyone** group and select **Read/Write**.
7. Click **Share** and then click **Done**.

We now need to create a GPO to redirect the folders.
1. Open **Server Manager**, Click **tools** and select **Group Policy Management**.
2. In the left navigation pane right-click **Group Policy Objects** and select **New**.
3. In the New GPO box input a name such as 'Folder Redirection' and click **Ok**.
4. In the navigation pane right click your newly created GPO and select **Edit**.
5. In the **Group Policy Management Editor** window navigate to **User Configuration | Policies | Windows Settings | Folder Redirection**.
6. Right-click **Documents** and select **Properties**.
7. In the **Document Properties** box, on the **Target** tab, click the **Setting** drop-down arrow, and then select **Basic-Redirect everyone's folder to the same location**.
8. In the Target folder location box select **Create a folder for each user under the root path**.
9. In the Root Path text box you need to enter the server name and the shared folder created earlier. For example, \\myservername\my shared folder.
10. Click **Yes** in the warning box.

The Folder Redirection GPO can now be applied to the OUs.

Installing Software on Computers Using Group Policy Management

Group policy management along with Active Directory enables you to deploy software packages from the server. In an environment that has a large number of devices, it is extremely useful as it means that you do not have to install the software locally on each PC. The software can also be removed via Group Policy management.

In order to achieve this, a specific type of install file is required. Usually, an install file will be a '.exe'. For this task a '.msi' file type is needed. You may need to check with the software supplier that this type of file is available.

To enable the computers to access the MSI file it must first be copied to a shared folder on the server. Read\Write permissions for the correct Active Directory user group must be set. See the chapter Shared Folders and Mapped Drives for instructions on how to set up a shared folder and assign permissions for a group. When selecting an Active Directory group for this purpose the group Authenticated users will suffice. Authenticated Users is a group automatically created and applies to any user that has successfully logged on to a computer connected to the domain. Another option is to create an AD group and ensure that all the computers that you want to deploy to are added to the group.

Once the folder has been shared we can create the GPO.
1. Open **Server Manager**, Click **tools** and select **Group Policy Management**.
2. In the left navigation pane right-click **Group Policy Objects** and select **New**.
3. Give the GPO an appropriate name and click **Ok**.

4. In the navigation pane right click your newly created GPO and select **Edit**.
5. In the **Group Policy Management Editor** window navigate to **Computer Configuration | Policies | Software Settings**.
6. Right-click **Software installation**. Navigate to **New** and select **Package**.
7. Enter the path and name of the install file in the following format \\servername\sharedFolder\filename.msi
8. Select the deployment method:
    - **Published** – Makes the package available for the user to install and should be applied to a user OU.
    - **Assigned** – Will install the package on computer start-up and should be applied to a computer OU.
9. Click **OK** and apply the GPO to the OU – Right Click the OU and select **Link an Existing GPO**.

DNS and DHCP

Within a home network, these settings largely go unnoticed as they are managed automatically by the router. Within a larger network, it is essential that these settings are configured correctly. Networks large enough to use AD should consider configuring these settings on the server to allow for centralised troubleshooting, management, and integration with AD.

DNS

DNS stands for Domain Name Service and is primarily used to link hostnames that are meaningful to users, such as www.google.com to an IP address. Computers only understand IP addresses and it would be tricky for us to remember or recognise lists of IP addresses. As such DNS is used to translate between the two.

When installed on a windows server, DNS uses a database or file to list domain names and their corresponding IP addresses. When a user types in a domain name or URL into a web browser the browser will attempt to match the domain name to an IP address.

Firstly the browser will check the computer's own cache and hosts file. If no record is found it will query the DNS server. The DNS server will then provide the client with the IP address so that the browser can contact the web server. If the DNS server does not know, it will query another DNS server and store the new information in its list. In this example, we have focused on opening a web page. A similar series of events are usually followed when requesting access to resources on the local network or Active Directory, with the only difference that the local DNS server is aware of all internal hosts and domains.

DNS servers can perform forward or reverse lookup. Forward DNS lookup is used to convert the domain name to an IP address, reverse DNS lookup works in reverse, converting IP addresses to domain names. Forward lookup is commonly used for web and service access. Usually, reverse DNS lookup is only used for network troubleshooting.

Setup and Configure DNS on Windows Server

To utilise this feature, the DNS Server role requires installation. Follow the tutorial on Installing Roles and Features on Windows Server and select the DNS Server role. Note that there is an option to install this role on the installation of Active Directory Users and Computers so you may already have it installed. Open server manager to see if it is available before proceeding with the installation.

In order to complete the configuration, you may need to contact your internet service provider (ISP) for the IP address of their DNS server and your network ID.

1. Within **Server Manager** click the **tools** menu and select **DNS**.
2. Open the **Configure DNS Server Wizard** by right-clicking the server name in the left navigation pane and select **Configure a DNS Server....**
3. The next page has 3 options
   - **Create a forward lookup** zone – This enables the standard function of resolving names to IP addresses.
   - **Create forward and reverse lookup zones** – In addition to the standard function, it also enables the function to resolve IP addresses to names. This can be useful when

troubleshooting and is the option that I would recommend for most networks.

- **Configure root hints only** - This will not create a database of name records for lookups, but rather will just have the IP addresses of other DNS servers where records can be found. I would not recommend this option unless you fully understand it.

4. On the following page select **Yes, create a forward lookup zone now** and click **Next**.
5. The next page has 3 options. If this is your 1 and only DNS server select **Primary Zone**. Click **Next**.
6. On the next page enter a zone name followed by '.local'. eg myzone.local. Click **Next**.
7. Name the zone file. I would advise leaving this as the default setting provided. Click **Next**.
8. Select **Do not allow dynamic updates** and click **Next**.
9. Select **Yes, create a reverse lookup zone now**. Click **Next**.
10. Select the **Primary zone** and click **Next**.
11. Select **IPv4 reverse lookup zone** and click **Next**.
12. Enter the network ID. If you do not this then your ISP may be able to assist. Also, check the IP address of the server or other devices for clues if the network is up and running.
13. Name the zone file. I would advise leaving this as the default setting provided. Click **Next**.
14. Select **Do not allow dynamic updates** and click **Next**.
15. Enter your ISP name servers, or use a DNS provider such as OpenDNS. If possible enter more than one server listed in case a DNS server is unreachable for some reason. The order forwarders are listed in is the order they are tried, so place your faster and most reliable forwarder at the top of the list. Forwarders are used if your DNS server ever gets a query for which it has no record, it can forward that request on to another DNS server to see if it has the answer.
16. Click **Next** and **Finish**. The DNS server is configured and ready to use.

DHCP

DHCP stands for dynamic host configuration protocol. In order for computers to access the network and the internet, an IP address is required. DHCP is used to provide IP addresses to clients automatically as opposed to entering an IP address on each device manually.

The DHCP role running on a server provides centralised easy to manage flexibility for tasks that may be more difficult to administer if using a network router or switch for DHCP. DHCP also provides the client with additional IP addresses such as a subnet mask, DNS server, and the default gateway address. In addition to providing IP addresses, the DHCP role can be used for other tasks such as reserving IP addresses for specific devices including servers and printers.

DHCP Configuration

In order to utilise this feature, the DHCP Server role requires installation. Follow the tutorial on Installing Roles and Features on Windows Server and select the DHCP Server role.

You will require the network IP address range, subnet mask and the IP address of the default gateway (router). If you do not know these your ISP may be able to assist you.

1 of the 3 IP address range classes shown below will likely apply depending on the size of your organisation and the configuration of the network.

Class	IP Address Range		Subnet Mask	Mask Length
A	10.0.0.0 10.255.255.255	to	255.0.0.0	8
B	172.16.0.0 172.31.255.255	to	255.240.0.0	12
C	192.168.0.0 192.168.255.255	to	255.255.0.0	16

In this example, we will use a class A IP address range. We shall designate the first 200 available IP addresses for DHCP. We shall then reserve the first 30 addresses from DHCP for devices such as servers, printers, and routers that require a static IP address. We shall use a default gateway or router address of 10.0.0.1.

Note that there is more than 1 method for excluding IP addresses from the DHCP scope. They can be omitted from the scope specified for DHCP or addresses within the scope can be reserved. Also, note that a Scope is simply a range of IP addresses.

1. Within **Server Manager** click the **tools** menu and select **DHCP**.
2. In the left pane select and right-click the name of the server and select **Authorize**.
3. Right-click the server name again and select **Refresh**. The icons next to IPv4 and IPv6 will change to green.
4. Select and right-click IPv4 and select **New Scope**.
5. Click **Next** on the welcome page.
6. Enter a scope name and click **Next**.
7. If you are following the example enter a start IP address of 10.0.0.1 and an end IP address of 10.0.0.200. Enter Length: 8 and Subnet Mask 255.0.0.0. Click **Next**.
8. On the **Add Exclusions and Delay** page enter a start IP address of 10.0.0.1 and End IP address 10.0.0.30 to exclude the first 30 address from DHCP. Click **Add**. Leave the **subnet delay in millisecond** as 0 if this is your only DHCP server. Click **Next**.

9. Review the default lease duration limit which should suffice in most cases and click **Next**. This is the length of time that a client will be given an IP address.
10. Click **Yes, I want to configure these options now** on the Configure DHCP options page and click **Next**.
11. On the **Router (Default Gateway)** page enter the IP address. In some cases, this will be the first usable address in the network so in this example we will use 10.0.0.1. Click **Next**.
12. On the following page if you have configured the DNS server the IP address should already be listed under the IP address column. Check the address and click **Next**.
13. Click **Next** on the **WINS Server** page. This is for older Windows versions and should not be required.
14. On the next window select **Yes, I want to activate this scope now** and click **Next**.
15. Click **Finish**.
16. Right-click the server name in the left pane and click **refresh**.

In the left pane under the server name and IPv4 the newly create scope should be listed. The options previously set can easily be modified by right-clicking the scope and selecting properties.

Click the drop-down list to show the available settings.

- **Address Pool** – The IP addresses available for leasing will be displayed here along with any exclusions that have been set. Additional exclusions can be added by right-clicking Address Pool and select New Exclusion Range.

- **Address Leases** - Displayed here are the clients that have been assigned an IP address by the server. The client can be assigned/reserved an IP address by right-clicking it and selecting Add to Reservation. Clients can also be added to a filter to deny them access in the future by right-clicking the client and selecting Add to filter. The lease can also be deleted if required.

- **Reservations** – Listed here are the clients and their IP addresses that have been reserved as above. Reservations can be made from here if you have the device's MAC address.
- **Scope Options** – The settings that are applied to the clients from this scope. If you have a very large environment you may have more than 1 scope.
- **Policies** – Rules can be applied to types of users or clients for example.

You are now ready to configure the clients for DHCP.

Shared Folders and Mapped Drives

Shared folders are usually located on a server and provide a central location for users to access files and documents. Along with Active Directory, you can control which users can and cannot access specific shared folders. Mapped drives allow the user to access the shared folder as if it were a locally installed drive.

In this example, we will create a shared folder and share it with an Active Directory group. We shall then provide access to the shared folder by creating a GPO in Group Policy Editor that maps a drive on the client machine.

In order to share folders, the File Server role is required which is installed by default on Windows Server 2016.

Firstly we will create a shared folder and allow an Active Directory group to read and write to the folder.
1. Open **file explorer** and navigate to the drive or folder that you would like to store the shared folder.
2. Select the **Home** tab at the top of the pane and click **New Folder**.
3. Name the folder appropriately and press enter.
4. Right-click the folder, click **Share** with and then click **Specific people**.
5. In the File Sharing box type the name of the Active Directory group that you would like to grant access, then click **Add**.

6. Click the drop-down arrow for the group and select **Read/Write**.
7. Click **Share** and then click **Done**.

Shared folders can also be created via Server Manager. Navigated to Server Manager | File and Storage Services | Shares. Click the drop-down arrow next to Tasks, select New Share and follow the wizard.

We shall now create a GPO to install the mapped drive.
1. Open **Server Manager**, Click **tools** and select **Group Policy Management**.
2. In the left navigation pane right-click **Group Policy Objects** and select **New**.
3. In the New GPO box input an appropriate name and click **Ok**.
4. In the navigation pane right click your newly created GPO and select **Edit**.
5. In the Group Policy Management Editor window navigate to **User Configuration | Preferences | Windows Settings | Drive Maps**.
6. In the Drive Maps pane right click in the white area and select **New** and select **Mapped Drive**.
7. In the **New Drive Properties** window:
   - In the **Action** dropdown list select **Create**.
   - Enter the location of the shared folder in the following format \\servername\shared folder name. To find the location navigate to the shared folder, right-click it, select **properties**, click the **Sharing** tab and the location will be displayed under **Network Path**.
   - In the Label as box you can enter the name. This is the name that will appear on the client. You can leave this empty and the folder name will be used as default if you prefer.
   - Select **Use** in the Drive Letter box and specify a drive letter. Avoid using C, D or anything else that is likely to be in use.
8. Click **Apply** and click **Ok**.

The GPO can now be applied to an Organisation Unit.

1. Locate the Organisational Unit to which you would like to apply the GPO within **Group Policy Management**.
2. Right-click the Organisational Unit and select **Link an Existing GPO....**
3. Select the Group Policy Object that you would like to apply.
4. Click **Ok**.

Shared Printers

Windows server enables you to set up and configure printers that can then be shared. This allows for centralised management and troubleshooting. Once a printer has been shared it can be accessed by multiple clients across the network.

For this tutorial, I have made 2 assumptions. The first assumption is that a printer capable of connecting to your local network is to be installed. Nearly all modern printers have the ability to connect to a network. The second assumption is that you have the necessary drivers for the printer. The drivers may have been provided with the printer on a disk or may be available to download online. Consult your printer documentation if you are unsure.

In order to utilise this feature, the Print Server role requires installation. Follow the tutorial on Installing Roles and Features on Windows Server and select the Print Server role. Note that this role is a sub-role of Print and Document Services. On the server roles page, you first need to select Print and Document Services. Following this, you can select the Print Server role for installation.

I would highly recommend using a static IP address for the printer. This can be done one of two ways. DHCP can be used to provide the printer with an IP address which can then be reserved using the DHCP server role. Or, an IP address can be manually entered into the printer using a valid IP address that has been excluded from your DHCP scope. Whichever method you decide to use make a note of the IP address and ensure that the IP address is either reserved or excluded from your DHCP scope.

1. Open **Server Manager**, Click **tools** and select **Print Management**.
2. In the left navigation pane under **Print Servers** right-click the server name and select **Add Printer** to open the **Printer Installation Wizard**.
3. As we are installing a network printer select **Add a TCP/IP or Web Services Printer by IP address or hostname**. Click **Next**.
4. In the **Hostname or IP address** text box enter the IP address of the printer. Click **Next**.
5. The server will attempt to locate the printer and search for the appropriate drivers. If the drivers are not found select **Install a new driver**, click **Next** and select **Have Disk**. Browse to the driver location and select the .inf file after you have extracted it from the zipped folder.
6. If the correct drivers have been found, ensure the printer name matches the make/model of your printer.
7. I would advise renaming the printer to something shorter and more meaningful. Eg 'Colour-ITsuite'. Click **Next** and the Server will install the driver.

8. Ensure that the option to **Share the printer** is selected and enter a share name for the printer. Again, I would suggest something short and meaningful.
9. Click **Next** and click **Finish**.

Group policy can now be configured to share the printer with clients.

1. Open **Server Manager**, Click **tools** and select **Group Policy Management**.
2. In the left navigation pane right-click **Group Policy Objects** and select **New**.
3. In the New GPO box input an appropriate name, such as the name of the printer, and click **Ok**.
4. In the navigation pane right click your newly created GPO and select **Edit**.
5. In the **Group Policy Management Editor** window navigate to **Computer Configuration | Policies | Windows Settings | Deployed Printers**.
6. Right-click and select **Deploy Printer**.
7. Enter the shared path to the printer eg \\servername\printer and click **Add**. Click **OK**.

The GPO can now be applied to an Organisation Unit.

1. Locate the Organisational Unit to which you would like to apply the GPO within **Group Policy Management**.
2. Right-click the Organisational Unit and select **Link an Existing GPO....**
3. Select the Group Policy Object that you would like to apply.
4. Click **Ok**.

Updating Computers Using WSUS

WSUS stands for Windows Server Update Services and enables you to manage computer updates and hotfixes centrally from your Windows server. The advantages of using WSUS are that you are able to control what gets updated and when; you can check which devices need updating and investigate any issues; you can choose the correct updates for your software; and it reduces internet bandwidth usage as only 1 instance of the update will need to be downloaded from the Microsoft Servers rather than every computer on the network using the internet to download the same file.

In order to utilise this feature, the Windows Server Update Services role requires installation. Follow the tutorial on Installing Roles and Features on Windows Server and select the Windows Server Update Services role. Prior to the installation, you will be presented with the following options.

- WID Connectivity – this stores the WSUS database on the same server that you are installing the WSUS role. Choose this option if this is your only server.
- WSUS Services – Ensure this is selected.
- SQL Server Connectivity – select this option if you have an additional server running an SQL database for WSUS.

In the next window of the role installation wizard, you will be required to enter a file path for the WSUS files and database. This folder can grow in size quite rapidly. If possible avoid using the same drive as the Operating system (C:). Enter a local file path with an available drive or partition and a suitable folder name such as F:\WSUS Files.

Leave the role services options required for this role as the default settings. Once the installation has completed follow the steps below to configure WSUS. We shall then go onto creating a GPO to enable WSUS on the client computers.

1. Start the **WSUS Configuration Wizard** by selecting **Tools** and **Windows Server Update Services** from **Server Manager**. Click **Next**.
2. Uncheck **Yes, I would like to join the Microsoft Update Improvement Program**. Click **Next**.
3. If this is your first or only server select **Synchronize from Microsoft Update** and click **Next**.
4. Ensure that you have internet connectivity, click **Start Connecting** and click **Next**.
5. Select ONLY the language or languages that you require updates for. Selecting all languages will require a lot of disk space. Click **Next**.
6. Select the products that you would like to support. Browse the options and choose the relevant products to your environment. Again I would not recommend selecting everything. Click **Next**.
7. On the **update classifications** page select the desired options. If you are unsure as to what to choose, leave the default options and click **Next**.
8. Choose **Synchronise automatically** and enter a time such as during the night when there are fewer users. 1 synchronisation per day should suffice in most cases. Click **Next**.
9. Check **Begin initial synchronization**. Click **Finish**.
10. The **WSUS console** now opens.

In the WSUS console, select your server to view the options in the drop-down menu.

- **Updates** – A view of updates available for install and updates can be approved or declined from here (see below).
- **Computers** – A list of the computers added to WSUS console.
- **Downstream Servers** – A list of any other servers configured for WSUS. In a single server environment, this will be empty.
- **Synchronisations** – View the Synchronization Status from the Microsoft servers. Ensure that the synchronisation was successful.
- **Reports** – Check the update status of the computers with various reports.
- **Options** – Change settings made in the initial WSUS deployment.

Prior to updates being downloaded, they require Approval in WSUS Console. Navigate to **Updates** -> **All Updates**. In the right pane select the updates, right-click and select **Approve**.

We shall now create a GPO in order to configure the WSUS settings on the client computers.

1. Open **Server Manager**, Click **tools** and select **Group Policy Management**.
2. In the left navigation pane right-click **Group Policy Objects** and select **New**.
3. In the New GPO box input an appropriate name, such as 'WSUS Settings', and click **Ok**.
4. In the navigation pane right click your newly created GPO and select **Edit**.
5. In the **Group Policy Management Editor** window navigate to **Computer Configuration | Policies | Administrative Templates | Windows Components | Windows Update**.

6. In the right pane double click to configure the following settings. Some of the options for the settings below are suggested for the purpose of this tutorial. Options shown can be changed to your own preference. Read the settings description for further information.
   a. **Configure Automatic Updates** – Select Enabled. Set Configure automatic updating to 4 – Auto download and schedule the install. Set Scheduled install day to 0 – Everyday. Set Scheduled install time to your preferred time. Click Apply and click OK.
   b. **Enable client-side targeting** – Select Enabled. In the Target group name for this computer enter the text 'All Computers'. Click Apply and click OK.
   c. **Specify intranet Microsoft update service location** – Click Enabled and in all the boxes enter the server location in the following format replacing 'server name' with your server. http://servername:8530 Click Apply and click OK.
   d. These are the minimum settings required to enable WSUS. Check the other settings to see if your environment would benefit if they were applied.
7. The GPO can now be applied to the desired OU.

I would recommend periodically running the Server Cleanup Wizard. This can be found within the Options menu in WSUS console.

Backing up your Server

For the purpose of this book, we shall be focusing on the Windows Server Backup feature that is provided at no extra cost with modern versions of the Windows Server Operating System. It can be used to backup the full server, the system state, selected storage volumes or specific files or folders.

There are numerous 3rd party software solutions to back up your server in addition to cloud-based solutions. Third-party software may include additional features not included with Windows Server Backup. You may wish to research this option further and some of the more popular choices include:

- Symantec Backup Exec
- Acronis Backup and Restore
- Carbonite
- ShadowProtect
- Backup Assist
- MozyPro
- Veeam

You may wish to perform both third-party software and windows server backups alternatively for additional peace of mind.

Backup data needs to either be sent to an external hard drive connected via a USB cable, local network attached storage (NAS) or cloud storage offsite via the internet. The choice depends on the type and amount of data to be backed up, the budget and your personal preference. Where proprietary or sensitive information is an issue, local storage on external hard drives or NAS is the most secure and usually more cost effective depending on the amount of data. Cloud services usually require a subscription fee but often provide more flexibility and less manual administration.

I would recommend encrypting any external hard drives used for backing up. Windows BitLocker can be used to encrypt volumes and drives and is available on Windows 10 and modern windows server software.

Windows Backup Server feature requires installation. Follow the tutorial on Installing Roles and Features on Windows Server, select the Windows Deployment Services role and select the Windows Server Backup feature.

Backups can either be run manually at a time of your own choosing or you can set a schedule to run at a specific time on a recurring basis. This guide demonstrates how to perform a single manual backup. However, if you wish to schedule a backup simply select Backup Schedule in the Actions pane rather than Backup Once as described below.

1. Open **Server Manager**, Click **tools** and select **Windows Server Backup**.
2. From the Actions pane on the right-hand side, click **Backup Once**. This opens the **Backup Once Wizard**.

3. On the **Backup Options** page, click **Different options**. Click **Next**.
4. In the **Select Backup Configuration** page, click **Custom** and click **Next**.
5. On the **Select Items for Backup** page, click **Add Items**.
6. In Select Items, click the check boxes for the items that you want to back up. To back up just certain folders or files, expand the folder tree and select the items that you want to include. Ensure that you exclude the device that you wish to store the backup on. Click **OK**.
7. On the **Specify Destination Type** page, click **Local drives**. Click **Next**.
8. On the **Select Backup Destination** page, select the volume from the drop-down list that you want to use to store the backup. Ensure that it has enough free space.
9. On the **Confirmation** page, review and click **Backup**. The wizard prepares the backup set and checks the volume.
10. On the **Backup Progress** page, you can view the status of the backup

Computers

Computer Specifications

Operating System

In order to integrate a computer into a Windows domain and interact with a Windows server, your computers will require a Windows operating system. I would recommend the latest Windows Operating system, which at the time of writing is Windows 10. The following guides will focus on Windows 10 but much of what is documented here will still apply to Windows 7 and 8.

Form Factors

Netbook – Very small, thin, light and inexpensive laptop computers. Screen sizes are typically between 8.9 and 10 inches. Netbooks contain a fraction of hard drive space and processing power when compared to other larger devices. They often rely heavily on web-based software so a good wireless network and a broadband connection are required.

Ultra Portable Laptops – Very light and thin with screen sizes under 14 inches. These are designed for on the go users and have around 5-6 hours of battery life. They will generally be more expensive than a larger laptop of similar specification and will usually include fewer features such as physical ports.

Midsized Laptops – Larger and heavier than the previously mentioned devices. Screen sizes will typically be 14 to 16 inches. They are very common as they have a balanced mix of specification, features, mobility, and price. They usually include Wireless capability and an Ethernet port which can be very useful in business environments where users do not want to rely too heavily on a wireless connection. Their specification is typically enough to handle most software for business and home users.

Tablet PCs – Usually a small touchscreen device, between 7" and 10". Powered by an internal rechargeable battery and highly portable. External keyboards can be attached to some makes and models.

Desktop and Tower – These are the most popular form factor available as they offer good specification to cost balance. Desktops are usually placed horizontally on a table with a monitor sat on top. Towers are often the same as or similar to desktops and are vertically oriented and traditionally located on tables or floors. The big units are known as full-size towers. The small units are known as mini or micro towers. As they have spacious box parts and components are easily upgraded or repaired.
Small-Form-Factor – These are very small space-saving desktop PCs. They will usually be placed on a desk or some models can be mounted on a stand at the back of the monitor.

The choice of form factor will largely depend on how portable the PC needs to be and what ports, interfaces, and components are required. Ensure the PC has everything that is needed to fulfill its purpose. Generally the smaller and more portable the PC the fewer ports, interfaces, and components.

Storage, RAM, and CPU

There are two main types of internal storage for PCs. Hard Drives or Solid State Drives (SSDs). SSDs are more durable and perform better than Hard Drives. An SSD will also have a better login time. SSDs are however expensive in comparison. For example, a laptop with a 500GB Hard Drive will be within the same price range as a similar laptop with an SSD of 128GB. If the priority is performance over storage capacity I would recommend an SSD. Additionally, when it comes to PC performance Vs cost I would recommend prioritising an SSD above the CPU and RAM.

The more RAM that your PC has the better it will be able to cope with multiple tasks simultaneously. As a minimum, I would suggest 4GB RAM for general use. Similarly, the better the CPU the better and faster the computer will perform. Intel Core-based CPUs would be my personal recommendation. The i3, i5 or i7 depending on budget and performance requirements.

Please note that the recommendations are based on my own personal preferences and experiences with different PC specifications. This is not to say that you should dismiss other options that may be more suitable for your requirements.

Joining a Domain and User Accounts

In order to make use of the Windows Server services such as security features, Group Policy and WSUS the PCs need to be added to the domain.

1. Open **File Explorer** by clicking the yellow folder on the taskbar at the bottom of the screen.
2. In the left pane right-click **This PC** and select **Properties** to open the **System window**.
3. Towards the bottom right of the **System window** click **Change settings**.
4. Click the **Change** button.
5. Select **Domain** and enter the name of the domain eg domain.local
6. Enter the domain administrator username and password and click **ok**.
7. A welcome message will appear, click **ok**. It will then request a restart, click **ok**.
8. Close the **system properties** window and click **restart now**.

Now that the computer is attached to the domain there are 2 options for logging onto it. A local account can be used that has been set up on the computer. Or users with an active directory domain account can log in.

To login with a local account enter the name of the computer followed by a backslash and the username and enter a password eg 'computername\username'.

To log in to the domain select Other user on the bottom left of the login screen and enter a username and password that has been created in Active Directory.

For certain types of users that use the same computer each time they log on, you may wish to create a local account for them and also add the computer to the domain. This enables the user to store their files and folders on the computer itself rather than transferring the data from the server each time they log on. As the computer is also attached to the domain the administrator is able to maintain centralised control of the computer for security and domain services. Users with devices that are required to be used offsite will also require a local user account unless a VPN has been administered.

Note that the same account used for the local account should also be added to Active Directory (with the same username and password) in order to enable the user to access resources such as shared folders and printers.

Follow the steps below to create a local user account.
1. In the **search box** on the taskbar type **settings** and select **Settings** from the results to open **Windows Settings**.
2. Select **Accounts**.
3. On the left of the page select **Other people**.
4. Select the **+** sign to Add someone else to this PC.
5. Select **I don't have this person's sign-in information**.
6. Select **Add a user without a Microsoft Account**.
7. Enter the username, password and security information for the user and click **Next**.
8. The account will now be listed and can be switched to a local administrator account if required by clicking the account name and selecting **Change account type**.

The user can now log in to the PC with a local profile and the PC can still access domain services as it is connected to the domain. At the login screen enter the computer name followed by a backslash and the username.

Mapping a Drive to a Shared Folder

Mapped drives allow the user to access the shared folder as if it were a locally installed drive. The two most common methods of configuring a mapped drive are via Group Policy or locally from the PC. Ensure that the user has the correct access privileges set in Active Directory in order to access the shared folder.

See the Chapter Shared Folders and Mapped Drives in the Server section of this book for further information on configuring shared folders and mapped drives.

To install a mapped drive to a shared folder from the PC follow the steps below.

1. Click **File Explorer** in the taskbar.
2. In the left pane click **This PC**.
3. At the top of the window click the **Computer** tab to open the **menu options**.
4. Click **Map network drive** to open the **map network drive configuration** window.
5. Select a drive letter from the drop-down list and enter the shared folder name and location in the following format \\servername\shared folder name.
6. Click **finish**.

The shared folder will then open and will be listed on the computer as a network drive.

Installing a shared printer

As with mapped drives shared printers can also be configured via the server through group policy or from individual computers.

See the Shared Printers in the Server section of this book for information on setting up and configuring shared printers.

To install and connect to a shared printer from a PC follow the steps below.

1. Click in the **search box** on the taskbar and search for **Control Panel**, press enter to open the **control panel**.
2. Ensure that the View by drop-down list towards the upper right is set to **Category**.
3. Click **View devices and printers** located below the **Hardware and sound** category.
4. Click **Add a printer** located towards the upper left.
5. Click **The printer that I want is not listed** located below the progress bar.
6. Choose **Select a shared printer by name** and enter the share name of the printer in the following format \\servername\printername and press **enter**.
7. Click **Next** and click **finish**.

Local Area Networks (LANs)

A LAN is a network of computers and other electronic devices that covers a small area such as a room, office, or building. In order for devices to access the server resources, they must be connected via the LAN. The majority of LANs will use Ethernet, Wifi or a combination of both to enable devices to communicate with each other. Ethernet is a network protocol that controls how data is transmitted over a LAN. Wifi uses radio waves to connect computers to Wireless access points.

A LAN network requiring a large wireless coverage will comprise of cabling, switches, routers, WAPs (Wireless access points) and wireless management systems. A physically smaller area or building may only require a single Wifi connection. In this scenario, a wireless management system will not be required.

Ethernet Cabling

Most laptops, desktops, and servers are provided with a standard RJ45 port used for plugging in Ethernet cable connectors. However, the cables themselves can vary. The main variations are the speed of data transmission and whether the cable is shielded. The maximum recommended Ethernet cable length is 100m and the category of cable will usually be printed on the cable.

Twisted pair (TP) refers to the internal wiring inside the cable. Pairs of wires are twisted around each other to reduce crosstalk. Twisted pair copper comes in shielded an unshielded forms. Shielding a cable helps to prevent electromagnetic interference and crosstalk. A shielded copper cable includes a protective conductive coating such as braided strands of copper, copper tape or a conductive polymer.

When looking to install Ethernet cabling consider the types of Ethernet cable available. Also, consider whether flame-resistant cabling may be required.

Cat 3 – This was popular in the 1990s and may still be found in some legacy networks. No new network installation should use this type of Ethernet cable. It is an unshielded twisted pair cable used for voice and can handle speeds of up to 10Mbps.

Cat 5 – This overtook Cat 3 as the primary choice around 2000. It is used for network speeds of 10 or 100 Mbps. It is unshielded and has largely been replaced by Cat5e as the primary choice.

Cat 5e – Category 5 cable was revised, and mostly replaced with Category 5 Enhanced. Cat5e is the most widely used Ethernet cable available. It is backward compatible with Cat5 and Cat 3 so can be used in most upgrades and new installations. It works for 10/100Mb and 1000Mb (or Gigabit Ethernet). Cat5e is unshielded and often used when large quantities of cables are required, such as lots of PC connections back to a single switch. This is because the cabling is economical, it is capable of 1000Mbps and it is easy to work with. Cat5e is suitable for most LAN installations.

Cat 6 – Also backward compatible with legacy Ethernet networks and is suitable for 10/100Mb and 1000Mb networks. However, Cat 6 has better transmission performance particularly for 1000Mbps speeds when compared to Cat 5e and is capable of 10Gb speeds when cable lengths are below 55 meters. This is because it is less prone to crosstalk. Cat 6 is suited toward environments where crosstalk is likely to be an issue. This includes areas that have lots of interference from things like power lines, lights, and manufacturing equipment. It may also be used for backend equipment such as a router to switch links. It is generally more expensive and more difficult to install when compared to Cat5e as it is thicker. Cat 6 can be shielded or unshielded.

Cat 6a offers 10Gb Ethernet to 100 meters as it has stronger shielding compared to Cat 6.

Cat 7 – This is a relatively new type of cabling and isn't used much as yet. It is very stiff as the pairs of internal wires are shielded as well as additional shielding around the entire cable. The shielding needs to be grounded and special connectors are required in order to make use of the cable's high-performance capabilities. Cat7 can also support 10 Gbps, but laboratory testing has successfully shown its ability to transmit up to 40 Gb at 50 meters and even 100 Gb at 15 meters. It is suited for use in data-centers and large enterprise networks.

Crossover vs Straight – Ethernet cabling is almost always straight through. With a straight through cable, the internal wires all connect to the same pins on the plug at each end of the cable. They are used to connect devices such as computers and printers to the host device (usually a router or switch). With a crossover cable, the wires connect to different plug pins at each end. They are used to connect like for like devices such as a computer directly to another computer, switch to switch or router to router. However, most modern devices have auto-sensing technology that detects the cable and device and crosses pairs when needed.

Switches and Routers

The primary purpose of both Switches and Routers is to ensure that data being transmitted between computers reaches the correct destination. In order to achieve this, they use MAC and IP addresses respectively.

Switches usually have numerous ports and are used to provide a wired connection to the network devices such as computers, wireless access points, printers, servers and any other devices connected to the LAN. Different models of network switches support varying numbers of connected devices. Consumer grade network switches typically provide eight or fewer connections for Ethernet devices, while corporate switches typically support between 32 and 128 connections. Switches can be connected to each other to add a progressively larger number of devices to a LAN.

Switches are usually unmanaged or managed. Managed switches are often set up or configured using a command line, or web browser, based interface and have additional features and capabilities to ensure optimal network performance and security. An example of such a feature is a virtual LAN or VLAN configuration. A VLAN can be used to separate different types of network traffic such as voice or CCTV traffic. Other features may include prioritising certain traffic such as traffic from a particular computer or to a specific server. This means that a correctly configured managed switch can optimise a networks speed and resource utilisation. Unmanaged switches require little to no initial configuration in order to work and are typically used by home consumers or for very small office networks where there are less than 10 computers and wired connections are preferred to wireless. Hybrid switches are also an option for smaller businesses. Their interface is much simpler than what managed switches offer. They are effective for small VLANs but don't allow monitoring, troubleshooting, or remote-accessing to manage network issues.

Routers are primarily used to connect different networks. So in order to connect to the internet or a separate network within a large enterprise environment, a router will be required. In the majority of scenarios, the Internet service provider will supply a router for internet connectivity. For many small or home office networks a single wireless router, provided by the ISP, with several ports and wireless capability may suffice. However, no matter how small your organisation it is worth considering business grade routers. They provide increased reliability as they are more robust for heavy usage and have additional features such as guest WiFi access.

Layer 3 switches are also available and blend the internal hardware logic of switches and routers into a hybrid device.

LAN Switch Purchasing – What to Consider

Managed, Hybrid or Unmanaged - This depends on the size and future expansion possibilities of the organisation. A managed switch offers the greatest security, flexibility, and assists in future-proofing the network. Budget permitting a managed switch is always preferable. However, unmanaged and hybrid switches offer benefits when used in the right situation.

The number of ports - Consider the number of devices that the network needs to support and consider future developments. It is likely that more devices will be required at some point and it is better to have too many ports. Also, think about additional devices that may be added to the network such as CCTV cameras and IP phones.

Power Over Ethernet (POE) - Devices such as IP phones, CCTV cameras, and Wireless Access Points may require POE. A POE switch is a network switch that provides electrical power to the device via the Ethernet cable. Some switches have a combination of standard ports and POE ports.

Switch Speed - Gigabit or 1000Mbps interfaces are now standard for most computers and network equipment. Budget permitting a switch capable of 10/100/1000Mbps speeds is preferred for most scenarios. Larger organisations may wish to opt for a 10Gb switch.

Redundancy – Consider the scenario if a switch were to fail. Who and how would it affect the organisation. It may be beneficial to have more switches with fewer ports rather than say a single larger switch. This way if a switch were to fail the network can continue in some capacity.

Warranties and Support – Consider the length of warranty available. Also, take into consideration the level of support for configuring the device and troubleshooting or monitoring should any issues arise.

Wireless LANs

In a small building or single room office, with only a few wireless devices, a single wireless access point will suffice and will usually be a wireless router that also provides internet access. Where wireless access to a network is required in various areas of a building, numerous wireless access points (WAPs) will be needed. Wireless coverage from a single access point can vary depending on physical obstructions and interference so careful planning is required prior to installation. WAPs typically connect back to a POE switch via an Ethernet cable.

Wireless networks with numerous access points can either be managed or unmanaged. A managed network is preferable as it provides better connectivity for wireless devices. This is because a managed system automatically moves the device's connection to the access point with the strongest signal, ensuring that it always has the best possible connection. In an unmanaged system, the devices will remain connected to an access point until it loses the signal completely and only then will it move to the nearest access point. A managed system also provides other benefits and capabilities such as creating multiple wireless networks or SSiDs (Service Set Identifiers) or providing individual WiFi access accounts for each user. Managed systems require an additional device known as a Wireless Management System. Alternatives include cloud-based systems that enable configuration through a browser over the internet.

WiFi standards ensure compatibility between different manufacturers and devices. The main standards in release order are 802.11a, 802.11b, 802.11g, 802.11n, and 802.11ac. The newer standards generally offer faster data transfer rates and will be standard on most wireless devices. However, 802.11ac is relatively new and may not be available on all devices. WiFi products support earlier standards to ensure backward compatibility and will automatically set to the best standard available between the Access point and the device. Multi-standard support will be labeled as something similar to 802.11b/g/n. In order to future-proof the network ensure that any new products are capable of 802.11ac.

Wi-Fi networks use radio signals in either the 2.4 GHz or 5 GHz frequency bands. 5GHz WiFi connections are generally considered to be faster and share the frequency with fewer devices, such as wireless cameras, microwaves, and mobile phones, so are less prone to interference. However, a 2.4GHz signal has more range and is more effective through walls and other solid objects. WiFi products that support both frequency bands are known as Dual Band. 802.11g uses 2.4 GHz frequency, 802.11n can use either frequency and 802.11ac uses the 5 GHz frequency band.

In order to prevent hackers snooping on wireless data as it was transmitted between clients and access points, encryption is required. During setup of a wireless router, access points or wireless manager there may be a choice of 3 encryption algorithms - WEP, WPA or WPA2. WEP (Wired Equivalent Privacy) was superseded by WPA (Wi-Fi Protected Access) and should not be selected as it has serious security weaknesses. WPA has been shown to have security flaws and has now been replaced by WPA2. Where possible WPA2 should be selected as it is currently the most secure choice, particularly when transmitting confidential personal or business information.

PSK stands for pre-shared key and refers to the WiFi passphrase. This along with the SSiD is used to create an encryption key. PSK would not be found in an enterprise network, instead, a RADIUS server would be used to hand out unique keys.

Within the WPA2 encryption protocol, there are two methods available for encrypting and decrypting information (known as a cipher) - Temporal Key Integrity Protocol (TKIP) and Advanced Encryption Standard (AES). To achieve optimal security AES should be selected as it is newer and the most secure. TKIP should only be used if incorporating legacy equipment is a necessity.

Licensing

Most PCs and other devices purchased individually are provided with a single device license for the Operating System. This also applies to most off the shelf software packages. Having a single license per device can prove to be problematic as organisations grow and more devices and software packages are required.

Microsoft offers a Volume licensing subscription option for businesses and educational establishments. Volume licensing subscriptions are usually purchased through a reputable third party supplier and are charged annually. Cost is dependent on the number of users.

The advantages of using volume licensing are:
- Microsoft Software and operating systems can be upgraded to the latest software available at no extra cost. You may wish to upgrade all devices to Windows 10 or the latest version of Office for example. When collaborating or sharing information it is important that users are using the same software across the organisation.
- There are different versions of Microsoft operating systems. For example, Windows 10 has numerous versions including Home, Pro, Enterprise, Mobile, and Education. Depending on the organisation you may require some of the features not available on some of the more basic versions. Volume licensing enables administrators to install or upgrade to, the required version with the necessary features. For example,

the ability to join a domain is not available in Windows 10 Home.

- 'Clean' OS installations can be made that do not contain additional unwanted software.
- Educational volume licensing offers other benefits such as permission to install Microsoft Office on students home or personal devices and Office 365 accounts.

When looking to purchase third party software or applications be sure to check system compatibility and licensing information.

Single user licenses - Most off the shelf software comes with a single user license that permits the software to be used by a single user on a single computer.

Multiple user licenses - A multiple user license allows more than one person to use the software. The permitted amount of users will be specified in the license.

Site licenses - A site license allows anyone on your business premises or establishment to use the software.

Anti-Virus

All computers need some form of protection particularly in places where there are lots of computers. Centrally managed anti-virus software is beneficial when administering numerous devices, as it enables administrators to monitor and resolve most issues without the need to check every computer individually.

Some examples of commonly used affordable anti-virus options for schools and small businesses are:

- Sophos
- Vipre
- Eset
- Webroot
- Bitdefender
- Symantec

It is worth noting that Windows 10 includes Windows Defender that offers anti-virus protection. Windows Defender does not require any installation as it is already integrated into the operating system.

Anti-virus software can often be obtained or purchased directly from the software company. However, suppliers and resellers may be able to offer advice and deals on the various options available.

Becoming an IT Technician

Course Recomendations

Nearly all companies and organisations use computers and many of them need someone to support their users and systems. Becoming an IT technician can often open the gateway to a long-term career where progression and promotion are often possible. There are many specialist IT roles that people work towards in order to develop their careers such as networking, security, server administration, web development, programming, computer science, and many more.

Many IT courses can be studied online in your own time and exams can be taken at testing centers, often these are local colleges. Ensure that your local testing center is approved. Check local colleges for classes, courses, and qualifications.

Whichever method of study you opt for, ensure to purchase the official book or guide for your course. It is possible to pass the exams by studying the course books alone if you wish (although I'm not recommending that). Udemy.com has various courses that cost very little. Check customer reviews and ensure the courses have been updated. Plurasight.com also offer courses for these certifications.

If you are new to IT, looking for a career change or just looking to expand your knowledge or CV and don't know where to start it can be very confusing. Here are some suggestions for courses and certifications.

- **CompTIA A+, CompTIA Network+, CompTIA Security+ and CompTIA Server+ Certifications** – These are entry level qualifications and courses designed to certify technicians with a foundational understanding of computers, computer networks, security, and servers. They are non-vendor specific and the perfect place to start if you have no previous experience or qualifications. Start with CompTIA A+ or CompTIA Network+ if you are not sure where to begin.

- **Microsoft Certification** – If you have some experience or prior knowledge you may wish to work towards Microsoft certification. Their entry-level certification is Microsoft Technology Associate (MTA) of which there are no pre-requisites. Microsoft qualifications are highly recognised within the IT industry and students can specialise in a category - Cloud, mobility, data, productivity, app builder or business applications. Each category has 4 levels – Technology Associate (MTA), Solutions Associate (MCSA), Solutions Expert/Solutions Developer (MCSE/MCSD) and Solutions Master (MCSM). Check the Microsoft website for more information. https://www.microsoft.com/en-gb/learning/certification-overview.aspx

- **Cisco Certification** – If you have some computer knowledge and have an interest in computer networking then you may wish to consider Cisco certification. The entry level courses are CCENT and CCT. Students can then work towards becoming an Associate (CCNA courses), Professional (CCNP courses), Expert (CCIE courses) and Architect (CCAr course). Cisco certification is also highly recognised and respected within the IT industry. See their website for more information. https://www.cisco.com/c/en/us/training-events/training-certifications/certifications.html

Entry Level IT Positions – Interviews

In addition to standard interview questions consider the following points and potential questions when preparing for an interview. For each potential question list 3 points.

- They may ask what you know about the organisation. Don't just think about IT. Study the organisation. What are they proud of? What are their achievements? Have they won any awards recently?
- They will likely ask you about what IT equipment that you would expect to see within their organisation. Try and get a rough idea about the size of the organisation and how many of their staff will be using computers. Are they likely to need network switches, a wireless LAN, and servers?
- They will ask you about previous roles and experience. If you are new to IT try and relate some of your previous responsibilities to the role for which you are applying. For example documentation and record keeping, working with and supporting colleagues or work prioritisation.
- They may ask about how you keep up to date with new technologies and technical information. Research any websites and/or publications that are relevant.
- They will likely want to know about your troubleshooting skills, how you might go about trying to resolve issues and how you dealt with a challenge. Think about specific examples of where you overcame a problem and the process that you went through in order to resolve it. They will want to know that you can remain patient, calm and methodical in your approach when faced with a challenge. An example of a specific question you may be asked is "What would you do if a computer was not connecting to the network?"
- They may ask technical questions specific to the role. Research the role thoroughly and gather information about specific tasks or jobs that you are likely to be carrying out. For example, questions for an IT technician role might be something like "What is DHCP?" or "What are the disadvantages of using imaging software?"

Conclusion

I really hope that this book has been of value to you and I would like to thank you for your purchase. The aim was to summarise all that I have learned over the last few years in my IT role and I believe that, on starting the role, I would have very much benefited from a guide such as this.

If you have found it useful I hope that you can take the time to leave me a quick review on Amazon.

I would like to wish you good luck with your IT system, exams, job role or any other endeavors that you sought assistance with from this book.

Thanks for reading.

Disclaimer

26338709R00045

Printed in Great Britain
by Amazon